Love

Investment, Intentionality, and Romance

Gerard Baptiste III

CONTENTS

Dedication

This book is dedicated to the love of my life, my confidante, and queen, Tiara. Our relationship and your love have taught me the true meaning of agape love. I've learned I can't always have my way, and I understand relationships are like a team, we all fulfil a role and duty and must support each other through both blessings and times of despair.

INTRODUCTION

Everything you want in a future mate and potential partner, go and become that. Check yourself daily. It's okay to take yourself out the dating game to improve your character and personality, ultimately for you to transform into the best version of your true, authentic self. Take time out to work on your flaws and insecurities so you don't scare away the person who you are destined to be with, even in marriage or a domestic partnership. Being in denial about your issues, character flaws, and insecurities will only delay and prolong the process of manifesting true agape (unconditional) love.

1

THE INFATUATION STAGE

"A.M.A.N.I."

A is for being amazed by your beauty

M is for the way you mesmerize me with the love in your eyes

A is for how I am amazed by your ambition

N is the way I can never get enough of your touch

I is for how I am intrigued by the beautiful and serene spirit you possess

A.

M.

A.

N.

I.

"One of a Kind"

More precious than a jewel found on the bottom

Of a deep blue sea

Oh, how I love how your soul

Connects with me

Confidence, boldness, and high self-esteem

Little did you know,

You are the woman of my dreams

Your energy is like a fresh fragrance

Flowing through a Parisian sky

It must be drugs,

The way you make me feel high

A slight bit of mystery,

I could see my destiny in your eyes

Oh, how I've longed for the day

When I could call you mine

No ruby, stone, or emerald

Could ever replace

The sweet memories we make,

Could never be erased

Rarer than an endangered species,

More exclusive than any ancient breed

Sailing into paradise,

Is where you belong ...

With me.

"ILLUSTRIOUS & MAGNETIC"

Infatuated with your touch

That gives me a euphoric rush

Sweet tender loving

From a woman that I love so much

Sent down from heaven,

An angel without wings

Only thinking of you

When a love song I sing

Magnetic radius,

Surrounding the circumference of your heart

Drawn into your illustrious eyes

Is where I must start

Never felt a love so true,

You ask, 'What do I mean?'

Imagination brought to life

Before my eyes, a reincarnated Queen!

No, not Elizabeth,

Not Nefertiti or Princess Diana

A woman that gives me fever,

Hotter than a summer in West Atlanta

I feel like a kid,

Digging into a box of snacks for a prize

Women, you don't understand,

How much of a blessing you are to my life

"BEAUTY IS HER NAME"

A rose could never capture all your essence,

The beauty you embody,

Is something so serene and surreal,

I pinch myself to see if it's true,

God truly took his time when he created you,

An angel chiselled by clay in the master's hand,

That somehow landed amongst mere mortals,

Long enticing legs,

That distract me every time you walk by,

Full lips that I daydream about,

Kissing me passionately while I close my eyes,

Dreaming of our future together,

Ascent so fragrant,

Smelling like a mixture of fresh linen, lavender, and fresh sun-flowers,

A gaze so crucial,

That every time I look in your eyes,

My heart begins to flutter and skip a beat,

Beautiful almond-caramel skin,

Slightly covered by tattoos,

The perfect mixture of urban and sophistication,

Beautiful eyes that hide pain,

But show tremendous femininity,

And show me resilience that inspires me,

A chiselled frame,

That could easily belong to an Olympian, Gold Medallist, or Track Star,

Slight curves, that could distract even the most faithful and devoted man as you walk by,

Energy that is so fervent and vibrant,

That it makes me nervous, excited, and inspired simultaneously

Beautiful hair, the perfect shoulders,

And the sweetest voice, reminding me of hummingbirds singing
and communicating

As dew drips on the grass and as clouds dissipate,

In the morning sun on a summer day,

I longed for this love,

Days when I argued with mates that were not destined to be part
of my future,

A touch of sensuality, vivaciousness, and tenacity,

That touched the very depths of my soul,

And had me addicted from the very first time

That I lied eyes on you...

Who knew I could experience a love so true?

Beauty is her name

"With You"

Being with you every day, is like a dream that has become reality. I enjoy the laughter, love, and happiness you bring to my life and the only thing that's missing is waking up to your beautiful smile each day.

"You Are"

You are the most interesting, sexy, caring, compassionate, and understanding person I've ever met and I'm glad you are a part of my life bae.

"My Angel"

When you sleep, you look like a cute, peaceful, and serene angel. I long for the day when I can fall asleep next to you every single night.

"CAPTIVATING THOUGHTS"

A desire to develop a close connection with an intriguing soul,

That so easily captivates my attention,

So high off love,

Like a drug,

It takes my soul to a new dimension.

At first, I was fearful,

Feeling it was too good to be true,

A relationship filled with abundance and vitality,

Compared to the others that left me feeling so blue.

I try to keep my composure in your presence,

But being around you makes me feel like a giddy six-
teen-year-old boy,

Because of your mysterious, classy, and elegant essence.

A love connection so deep it's bonded like an anchor stuck at the
bottom of a deep blue sea,

No matter what they say,

I will not allow obstacles to come between you and me,

Or should I say, 'You and I?'

Blossoming like a garden, touched by sweet due in the morning
sunrise,

The previous seasons of my life have ended,

But somehow, with you, I have arrived.

Hypnotized by curly brown hair, and the gaze of love in your
enchanting brown eyes,

I'm a man with many dreams,

But the sweetest one comes true, with you,

Every day that I'm alive.

"I Admire You"

I admire you so much for your resilience and fortitude during this season of your life. I am always here for you, and never forget that bae. I've got your back and the type of love I have for you will endure through all seasons. I believe in you, and more importantly us, and I am always going to fight for us no matter what life may throw our way.

2

ROMANCE

"More Than I Can See"

Maybe it's your spirit I see when I look into your eyes

More than a Queen more like an angel in my eyes

Power in your words, the truth comes from your lips

The passionate type of woman I could never forget

The image of a soldier, someone always down to ride

Who hears what I have to say and is always by my side

A match made in Heaven, something only God could ever plan

My heart runs from truth and takes me to a distant land

A place of harmony, passion, love, a foundation for our plans

Every breathe I take just gives me another chance

To treat you like a Goddess and show you sweet romance

I've played so many games how I could ever deserve,

A woman so gorgeous that I would never try to hurt

I long for your love but I control my emotions

We walk side by side, to spend time and devotion

Your soul is more than I can feel, and more than I can see

To keep me wishing to be the man, that everyone would want to be

What I have is so precious, what I have is so true

If I had enough time, I would give it all to you...

Beautiful Love, My Sweet Love

"INNER BEAUTY"

What I love most about you is not just how cute and beautiful you are,

But that you have a strong inner beauty that is as radiant as the Pacific sun.

When I look at your character, I see longevity,

When I look into your eyes, I see humanity,

When I look at your life, I see humility,

And most importantly, when I look at your heart, I see a key.

The key to mine.

3

My Love is Real

"Five Things I Love About You"

(My Bae)

1. Your smile, (you do this cute thing with your lips when you smile)

2. Your body, I love how well you take care of yourself and your health

3. Your authenticity and sincerity

4. You have legs for days that are hypnotizing

5. The sexy way you walk

"The Love You Dream Of"

Your beauty is as radiant

As the Tuscan sun

If you are in search for Samson, or a king like Solomon,

Baby, I am the one

A touch of compassion,

Hidden mysteriously behind my eyes,

I'm a wild April 1980s baby,

Are you sure you're ready for the ride?

Sometimes I will provoke

Pieces of my heart,

That have rarely been touched

If I told you, "You are my destiny!"

Would I be saying too much?

I'm not sure what tomorrow holds,

But I'm sure it will be full of splendour,

I know you are used to men

Being harsh As a Chicago Winter,

I'm so different from them,

Baby, can't you see?

I'm secure enough,

To introduce you to the vulnerable parts of me

I can cover your wounds,

Like a band aid,

And make your heart feel better

With so much heart every day,

No cardiologist could ever measure

I'm secure enough

To profess my love,

Without a second thought

And to never return or take back

Any gift that I've bought

My love cuts deep like a machete

It's so far from petty

It could last a lifetime,

Are you sure that you're ready?

Your friends tell you,

"He's too good to be true, Girl,

He's not what he seems!"

But truth be told,

I already know...

I'm the man of your dreams

TIARA - HAPPY VALENTINE'S DAY

More beautiful than a bouquet of roses,

Possessing the ability to simultaneously captivate my heart and
mind with light-speed

Smelling fragrant like a Tuscan field full of white lilies,

Whiter than the coat of doves,

I hope you accept this teddy bear and roses,

And just know it's covered in love

"Our Connection"

There is a feeling that is immeasurable

When I'm deep in your warm embrace

A feeling of joy

When we meet face to face

Heart palpitations

And flashes of nervousness

Like, again, I'm thirteen years old

Oh, what a treat I would be missing,

If I allowed my Ex to make my heart turn cold,

When our lips touch

If feels like something divine

I see glimpses of my destiny

That pass through my mind

Me and you united

With love we take a new route

I find myself making plans

And I can't keep you out,

The body of a goddess

That somehow landed on Earth,

Connected by attraction

In your vibration, I immerse

If I'm the captain of your ship,

I won't let it submerge,

At a time that was so bleak,

I didn't think admiration could occur,

But then this beautiful, brown woman

Somehow caught my eye,

It somehow made me a better man,

I can't lie

When I think of you,

I get a warm chill, that I just can't ignore,

And I love how you've taken me to new heights,

Maturing in ways that I never did before,

It's so divine,

Life would feel stagnant without you,

I try to play it cool,

But the truth is, I'm crazy about you

The next level requires a co-captain,

To guide me behind the wheel,

And when I'm in your presence,

It feels like time stands still

"Every Day You Amaze Me"

(Pt. 1)

Words can't express how I feel about you,

No amount of money can be equivalent to the amount of love I have for you,

You might ton understand how your beauty and resilience inspire me,

It gives me the will to keep moving forward, face my fears, and tackle my problems head on,

I have never experienced meeting someone who inspires me, who can be so attractive, but still durable through all the tough situations that life throws at us,

There's not a day that goes by,

That I don't think of your beautiful eyes,

That I daydream about your luscious lips,

That I'm mesmerized by your beautiful smile,

And I'm so easily hypnotized by your wit and your charm,

Your love fills me with gratitude,

It teaches me what the true meaning of sacrifice is,

And never misses the goal of amazing me,

You're the most thoughtful, talented, empathetic,

Caring, and selfless woman I have ever met, and you are the love of my life.

"Every Day, You Amaze Me"

(Pt. 2)

You are the most tenacious, yet tender, loving, caring, generous, supportive, attentive, and sexy woman I know...and every day you amaze me.

"My Love Stands Firm"

Should I like you, I should love you, all day I think of us and what we could be

But now my feelings are a mystery

I'm filled with passion & desire, but it seems like time has calmed that fire

Sometimes I write love songs to be romantic,

But see baby my heart endures all circumstances

Instead, I'm thinking what could and should happen,

But I will think of our fights and try to move past them

See my love for you is real, the opposite of plastic

That will stand strong, life-long through any disaster

I say I love you because you possess what I like

So let my words lift you up and let your mind take flight

My love is unconditional, it's more than just physical

And when I leave this Earth, I know you would miss it so,

I say this to be real, not egotistical

This bond between us is so strong, without it my condition is critical

See God made my body, and he made the blueprint

But you occupy my mind so much that it doesn't make sense

You require my attention; you got me in a new dimension

You possess the beauty of a queen that requires no extensions

So, when you think of Love, please remember my name

Let's be good to one another because I'm sick of these games

4

RELATIONSHIPS REQUIRE EFFORT

"Nothing Like Your Smile"

Pt. 3

Verse 1:

No other vowels matter,

Baby just you and I,

Relationship tested by the fire,

Feel like I'm crucified,

I sued to wannabe a playa,

Like Do or Die,

But I would be missing out,

If you weren't in my life,

Don't know many women,

35

Who would date and not change things,

Only to find out she's temperamental,

And struggles with the same thing,

I used to disappear,

To my corner of Atlanta,

Until I found someone who Cheers for me,

Like Ted Danson,

Jealousy and third wheels,

They're something like a Cancer,

My ex hitting up my phone,

I won't even answer,

She left thinking the grass would be greener,

You've got everything I've dreamed of,

So, she won't come between us,

I like how you're conservative,

And not about the turbulence,

It's crazy how your mother died,

Around the time I learned to live,

The past is not concerning me,

Burn it to the third degree,

Soon you'll see a better me,

Once I recover from surgery

Chorus:

When I think of black love,

Baby,

You are the one that I think of,

I love your smile, every time that we link up,

Nothing else matters, baby just us

(Repeat twice)

"PREPARATION"

(Preparing Us)

They say Proper Preparation Prevents Poor Performance,

I must learn to give my all,

And not to be docile and dormant

I fee like we are both being prepared for new levels

Where opportunities present temptation from a new devil

I learned being faithful is a good thing,

And if I want to be a successful husband,

And that if my Queen is not happy,

It doesn't matter if I have women by the dozens

I thought I was part of the game,

38

When I truly wasn't,

Picking up bad habits,

And pretending to be perfect in public

I spent years running away

From the possibly the best thing that happened to my life,

The only thing that would make it better,

Is if you'd be my wife,

We could grow together,

And take trips in luxurious cars,

Be fruitful and multiply,

And have as many grandchildren as the stars,

Maybe I'm thinking too hard,

I must slow down to make choices that are right,

Truth be told,

When I'm with you, I feel high as a kite,

We could take it step by step,

There is no need to rush,

We are both evolving,

So, God is Preparing Us,

A King without a fitting Queen,

Cannot succeed with his purpose in life,

Me with no You,

Is like a plant dying from lack of sunlight

"THE BEST ME, FOR YOU"

The truth is, I have been spoiled

I'm used to getting money fast, and spending money even faster

Obtaining what I want quickly,

Then losing it in a self-destructive disaster,

I exchanged numbers with you,

But what came after,

Is a brown girl,

Who filled my life with wisdom and laughter,

I've tried and failed,

My old ways won't prevail,

I'm used to playing so many manipulative games,

It's simply the truth, I hold myself accountable,

I am the one to blame,

Listening to some goofy dudes telling me, 'Because I have only one girl, I'm a simp and a lame.'

But you believe none of those tales,

You made me come correctly,

And approach you like a Queen,

When you get what you prayed and asked God for,

It's more rewarding than it seems,

I must work and be challenged,

To build an indestructible team,

Oh, how God blessed me,

With the woman of my dreams,

A love so tender,

I'm not afraid to be vulnerable,

It makes me smile in the morning,

No more bitterness,

Now I'm approachable,

As we reach another year,

Now my vision is clear,

Building a foundation is clearly my goal,

Now I must unlearn years of self-malice, jealousy, possessive-
ness, insecurities,

And manipulative control

5

PROTECT & PROVIDE

"Love is a Trip"

Love is a trip

It's a funny thing

First comes infatuation, then sensuality,

Then Contentment, resentment, and rage

Why do we guard our hearts so closely – Because we're truly afraid

That person your texting could be your future King or Queen,

But why do relationships have to be black & white,

With no grey in between,

Why can't this love belong to us,

And be selfish with no one else opinion

Why do I have to ask ten other people,

To make You & I decisions,

Truth is being faithful is a challenge,

I'm working to lose and bind a generational curse,

But I face temptation, when I see voluptuous women in tight
leggings and skirts,

If you only knew those, that came before you,

You might deny giving Daddy a try,

The truth is I use it to my advantage, that I'm a different and
mysterious guy

I've built these bad habits, of my player ways, over nearly a
decade,

It's hard for me to give only you my heart,

Because deep inside I'm afraid

True love is kind, patient, caring,

And not limited to temporary conditions,

If I could turn down the influence of my old ways, I could
complete this mission

Love is not selfish, and humble enough to admit when it's wrong

Truth be told, you will get your act together for the one who you truly belong

Love is a strong word,

Be careful how you use it

And baby girl, I love hard so if I give you my heart, please don't abuse it

"We Need to Talk"

We need to talk

I want to trust you,

But in many ways, I fear you will disappoint me

My expectations are too high,

My patience too low

I take things for granted,

And I just need to learn how to enjoy life

I'm confused, and perplexed

Hidden confessions of my bad decisions

I've been baptized and cleansed by your blood,

But I barely feel like a Christian

I've done many bad things,

And I've hurt many people that didn't really deserve it

They never really accepted me for who I am,

And it makes me feel so nervous,

Why can't you see past my robust exterior,

And just take me serious

If I told you I was in intelligent enough to be a doctor,

You would give me a look like you are delirious

I put a harsh mug on my face,

So, I could somehow disguise all this pain

I look forward to the sunshine,

But in a strange way I find comfort in the storms and through the rain

Beneath the surface,

I feel emotions I can't explain,

Is it really worth it with no one to call my own,

If through deceit I made many treacherous gains,

Broken bottles on the pavement,

Ashes from cigars that linger so distinctly on my clothes,

How can I gain a friend If I assume everyone is already a foe?

Bad relationships tarnished by ego, false expectations, and pride

Truly life has no purpose without a home, and a companion by my side

What does it really mean,

I took a shower but feel so unclean,

Tarnished by reckless habits and bad decisions,

Truth be told, what goes around comes around,

And I deserve this for the way I treat women,

You need someone that will cherish you,

And not exploit your garden for sensual pleasures,

You deserve the best,

And now I understand that one man's trash is another man's treasure

Wow, I really must do better

"Promises"

I promise to never abandon you,

And take you for granted, like he did

I promise you loyalty and affection,

And to keep your deepest secrets

To highlight your positive traits,

And not expose your weakness

I promise to treat you like a Queen,

Even on days that you forget your crown

I promise to be your rock, solid as granite,

And to pick you up when you fall

I promise to care for you,

Be by your side and to provide for you

To treat your heart carefully,

And not to split your heart in two

Promise to show devotion and affection,

Even for no reason,

To love you and treat you like a princess,

During all seasons,

I promise to be a protector & provider,

And to never leave you all alone,

And promise to pull my fair share,

Once I turn our house into a home

"He Had a Plan"

God knew what he was doing when he introduced us,

We were both captured in a time where our lives were headed in a different direction,

But somehow our hearts and our spirits are synchronized,

He sent me someone who matched my vibration,

With a beautiful smile, a gentle heart, and who possessed perseverance, truly all the qualities that I've ever wanted in a partner,

Just at a time when I was ready to throw in the towel, a gentle voice whispered to me, "Get back in the game, if you pass up on her you will be overlooking a blessing."

I wasn't sure what that meant at the time, but now destiny has answered all my questions,

Tragedy and trauma,

Seamlessly brought our fates together and taught us how to be true friends,

Now you're the love of my life,

And with you by my side,

No trouble can withstand,

I'm a living testimony of how a Queen can bring out the King qualities in a Man,

I promise to give a life full of love, adventure, and affection,

Babygirl, take my hand

"PRECIOUS AS A DIAMOND"

To me you are like a precious and rare diamond,

Made under pressure being prepared to shine in front of the world at the perfect moment.

When I see you, I embrace your flaws because to me that is what makes you so beautiful, so pure, genuine, full of love and authenticity, and somehow God knew you would be the perfect match for me.

I love your independence, your integrity, the way you care for others so selflessly, and the way you acknowledge me and accept me for who I truly am.

My plan is to spend many more years with you right by my side, and the only thing that could make our relationship better is me waking up to your mesmerizing eyes every morning.

You are my diamond babygirl.

"Never Forsaken"

You have a hypnotizing charm,

That sends my heart into a romantic trance

I've learned relationships take work and

Commitment, before you can advance

The nights I've longed for you,

Just to hold your hand,

Somehow my purpose feels more grounded,

Knowing you that I'm your man

No woman could ever duplicate

The way you made me feel,

How you were able to soften my heart,

Which was once hard as steel,

I felt lost like a ship,

Tossed by ocean waves to and from,

Because of deep commitment and dedication,

There are a few places I no longer Go,

I've worked tirelessly,

On a path to break generational curses,

I love how patient you are with me,

And how you contribute to my excursion,

Women try to infiltrate and get me to abandon

A love that's so genuine and true,

Trying to test if I really have deep devotion,

To a woman as captivating as you,

I once had my mind trapped in a system,

Surrounded by iron bars like a two-time felon,

God knew uniting us would keep me

From sliding into a deep depression,

The support you give, your tender care

Fills me with so much esteem,

It's you and I against the world,

I've noticed we make a great team,

A vision of God, embodied in a woman,

Who understands submission,

And I don't mind reciprocating it,

Because when I talk, you listen

You told me, "I love your eyes...

Because you look into my soul"

It's seldom that you find something so real,

That needs no manipulation to control,

With wisdom, we'll grow

And the bond we have will never vanish,

I love how you have self-respect,

And from me how you effortlessly command it,

Without a camera to capture,

One of my life's most beautiful scenes,

I will never forsake OUR captivating love,

Because you take time to

Understand the real ME.

6

Your Backbone in Times of Trouble

"Out of My Reach"

Tears on my pillow,

Tears dripping down my neck,

Times like these

Make me want to smoke a cigarette

When something hits you heavy,

And knocks you down to your knees

When your lover's mother

Suddenly dies, and the torment was not foreseen

Five weeks of torture,

When I couldn't feel your touch,

I've never thought of more I could do,

But in the moment, I couldn't do much

While you are worlds away

In a small town in Virginia,

I had pain and insecurity irritating me,

Like a wood chip splinter

In a way I couldn't do anything

To comfort your heartache & pain,

I had nothing to do with it,

But somehow, feel like I'm the one to blame

Maybe If I saw this death coming,

I could've prepared,

Why do bad things happen to good people,

It seems unjust and unfair

The best I could offer is a prayer for you,

And ask God to dispatch his angels

I've never dealt with this before,

And didn't know the right angle

Why do bad things happen to good people,

It seems unjust and not right,

But I know your mother is in heaven,

Proud and smiling,

As she looks down from the sky

"Arise"

I rise,

Rise above circumstances,

Rise above fear

But when I close my eyes then reopen them,

The same disaster appears

Filled with grief,

I need relief

But no one knows the depression

That festers beneath

I'm kind but it feels like in this race I'm in last place,

If people only truly know the resentment that fills my hearts space

Empty bottles of pills,

That lead to stacks of dollar bills,

I'm conflicted because poisoning my community,

Could make me rich for real

The pain is too intense, it seems unreal

If I could only drop all my mental and emotional baggage,

And melt this heart of steel

I cried out to my Lord, on my knees,

With buckets of tears falling from my eyes,

Sometimes I could see my grandmother's smile while I look into the sky

I try to be a kind soul, but I'm a Two-bit hustler in disguise

If people knew the real me, they would only grow to despise

I'm so far from perfect,

My itinerary is filled with lies

I'm stuck in a deep rut,

I can no longer live this lie,

As I reached for the box of tissues,

A voice whispered to me, 'Arise!'

"TRUE"

A true friend is someone

Who's there when you're in need

Someone not worried about benefits,

Through thick and thin,

When you have problems, they're there to provide advice,

And if you ever need a Favor, they never think twice

If I'm in trouble, I cast my cares on your shoulder,

Like Jesus of Nazareth with the Cross,

And if I ever lose the game, we both take a loss

No love lost,

But it's so perplexing, I can't figure it out

I want to learn to trust you, but I'm jaded with all this doubt

You still show me love,

Find Forgiveness, then we find a way,

I'm very close to the exit,

Could you please help me navigate the way

You tell me don't focus on the problems,

Or they will only be magnified,

I'm so used to being on my own,

I'm not sure what's it like to have a friend along for the ride

Right by my side,

Through all these insecurities that I perceive,

Wow, I've never known a true friend indeed

"LOVE IS RISKY"

A Letter to The Love of My Life

I understand the risks associated with relationships and love – you are giving the person you adore your trust and confidence that they will do the right thing, be loyal, and will not break your heart. I assure you that all my intentions are pure and genuine. I am nowhere near perfect, but I can learn to be the perfect partner for you. I promise to make you smile more than I make you cry; I promise to rub your back and feet on rough days and be encouraging to you. I will stick by your side every step of the way, and I look forward to building decades and a lifetime of memories and positive experiences with you. Just allow me to show you how much I adore you, in all the ways I can.

7

GROWING PAINS

Giving You a Better Me

"Ego is Dangerous"

Humility comes before honour,

Pride always proceeds a fall

Ego is a limitation that separates us all

Ego is the great divider that can make even the best of friends depart from one another

They say, 'Keep your circle small!' because if you must question their loyalty,

Then they don't need them around you

Why are the people that were spectators for round one,

Not here to help me fight Round Two?

I've figuratively and literally given folks shirts on my back,

And I gave them way too much trust,

I'm so puzzled why these people threw me under the bus

Here's a fact, real gratitude doesn't selectively forget good deeds,

I was the one you called when you didn't have shoes to cover your two feet

What I now understand at the age of thirty-five is that all men, women, and even children have flaws

And if I have it all, but have nothing to give, then there's no point at all

Greed will kill you,

Arrogance will create loneliness,

And Criticism is a double-edged sword we all need to learn to digest

"Elevation"

Nights filled with hunger

Days filled with desperation

I spent over a decade writing songs to vent frustration

So many spoils of success

The game lacks loyalty

So much money placed in material possessions

I undervalue my true loyalty

In a country, where values are based on your tax bracket

I swore to myself I would not be one to live

Devoid of my destiny, I lusted

For the things I've never experienced before

Wanting more than any hustler ever made

But I was distracted,

Because my focus was jaded

In a world, where the one thing we want most,

The dollar bill

Is dirtier than The Everglades

I became emotionally distant, reclusive, and my perspective became tainted

Tainted by the sorrows of yesterday, that were long gone

I started returning to a lifestyle I promised myself I would never accept again

Alcohol filled my nights,

Medicated with sedation kept the pain numb enough for me to endure,

Daily, in search for elevation,

I began meditation

"Oblivious"

How could I fathom this?

Getting things going, like a catalyst

Imagine if I was bolder,

Not timid or afraid,

Imagine if I was a rapper,

That only spoke of getting paid

I wrote many pages,

But couldn't read through the lines

I have sight,

But feel so damn blind

I loathe the fakeness,

Praying for my downfall,

As I arise

This is something I experienced when I was only twenty-two,

I thought Codeine Cough Syrup was my only breakthrough,

Alone in my home

Taking Hydrocodone,

Lost in a zone, where I lost track of time

I took two steps forward,

But feel two steps behind,

You came into my life, but had crooked intentions

Did 30 favors, and they weren't genuine

Blind to the jealousy,

Blind to the deceit,

I brought you all of me,

No return, No receipt

I brought you all of me,

No return, No receipt

"CRY NOW LAUGH LATER"

Tears soaking the pillow,

Too ashamed to show my face,

Some days I don't have the strength to run this race,

They say pressure creates diamonds,

And lifting weights produces muscles,

I wonder why the children of the sun

Must endure so much struggle

It's been over 400 years,

But master's whip still lashes our backs,

So don't ask me, "Why are you mad, and Why do you overreact?"

It's because television tells lies,

And courts treat us less than citizens,

It seems the only way to get rich is to

Become a rapper,

But we're smart enough to be physicists

I drive through the city,

And see an eerily similar pain on my people's faces,

It's hard to survive

In the home of the racists,

And to succeed we must hide our true nature,

And transform into Uncle toms,

They're just trying to feed their daughters,

That's why they carry crack cocaine in their palms,

So why should I give a damn about Israel or Palestine, or Ukraine
being hit by missiles,

When my little cousin gets bullied in school,

And to solve his problems he runs and grabs a pistol,

When my niece has no father figure or few role models in her
life,

And nowadays women are more like husbands,

And men are more like wives,

It seems so confusing,

These are very Perilous Times,

So I'm not waiting for them to hand me something,

I'm going to take and work for,

What I already know is mine.

"ALONE"

(Four Walls Closing In)

Alone, feeling like I'm in solitary confinement

Praying and meditating for my next assignment

Surrounded by people, but I feel like a foreigner

Entrapped in a state,

But I'm not talking Florida

Four walls closing in,

Followed by heart palpitations,

Even Adderall couldn't give me this level of concentration,

I feel like a broken down El Camino

With a plush and luxurious interior,

'Am I truly smart enough to become a doctor or scholar,

And why do they treat me like I'm inferior,'

Why is it when I level up,

People in my life begin to act insecure,

You must understand,

My blessings are our blessings,

And that's for sure

Kind-hearted,

But I'm surrounded by so much treachery,

But jealousy, manipulation, and monitoring spirits

Will not stop my destiny

Top Five Reasons Why You Are Perfect for Me

1. You go with the flow – it teaches me to relax, enjoy the moment and celebrate the small things

2. Your unconditional support

3. You don't try to be the 'Man' and the 'Woman' in the relationship

4. Your patience and humility

5. The sexy way you walk into the bedroom before we make love

Bonus:

The look of Love in your eyes when you look at me

"A Million Questions to Ponder"

There's beauty in the in-between phase. This is not a philosophical or ideological notion saying, 'to be complacent,' but to become grateful for what you already have. A great African proverb says, 'There's danger in eating your dinner in the morning.' In other words, there's a disservice you do to yourself by reaching or obtaining things before you can even handle the blessings that are right in front of your face. Ask yourself the following questions:

1. Have you really grown & developed?

2. Will you be kind to people who openly mock and gossip about you?

3. Will you remain loyal to that friend who needs emotional support when their parent is facing a terminal illness?

4. Will you smile and wave at people you sense are jealous of you?

5. Will you still love people despite them mocking your faith?

6. Will you be courteous and cordial towards people who only call you when they need something?

"Everlasting"

Look into your eyes,

I see the soul of a charismatic Queen that should be cherished, valued, and honoured with the best love that my heart is able to give.

There are ways you effortlessly inspire me to show up, conquer my fears, and tackle all of life's obstacles – because of your resilience, compassion, and honesty, which is a brilliant combination to combat the challenges life throws at us.

My vow to you is to be humble, noble, righteous, supportive, and respectful not only when things are going well between us, but even at times when we encounter adversity, life's difficulties, and hardships.

What lights up my morning every single day is the sweet thought of being loved by you.

How you lead with integrity and selflessness, even putting other's needs before your own.

It reminds me of the Agape or unconditional love I have developed for you over time, and it encourages me to keep growing each day.

My promise to you is to lead with integrity, authenticity, vulnerability, and benevolence and to communicate and express myself even if it's a difficult task to complete.

I want to be able to honour you with good decision-making, bless you with honesty, lead with integrity, love you unconditionally, and to always be myself around you, bae.

I love how you accept me where I am, and how you respect my unique qualities.

It inspires me to become the best provider and protector than I can be,

Transforming into the man God intended for me to be,

Building a beautiful kingdom with my rib & backbone, that will stand the test of time, with an enchanted soul like you, Babygirl.

"You Are Truly Priceless"

When I'm with you

Time stands still and it feels as if

Nothing else even matters

Who knew we would grow to have the type of love,

I can't even fathom

Something real,

That provides heat in the wintertime,

And a cool breeze on a summer night

No matter how dark the skies get,

When I daydream of your smile,

It turns my skies bright,

Every day that passes,

For me, is a constant reminder,

If I surely go looking for someone like you,

I would never find her

One of a kind,

Like a red stone found in Sierra Lione,

I wonder if you could feel my presence,

Like I feel yours when I'm all alone?

I feel like I'm at the carnival,

And I just won the raffle,

Someone once told me, "There's no need of working hard,

If you don't have someone to share your castle."

No dollar amount could ever equate

The depths of emotions that I feel,

For you my Redbone Princess, Tiara,

I've never felt something so real.

8

I Don't Care What They Say

"U & I"

I want the type of love

That can't be severed by gossip and rumours,

The type of bond so strong,

It continuously grows like a tumour,

Not confined by societal norms

Or other folks' opinions,

Something holier than matrimony,

You can feel God's presence when you mention

Many vowels are available,

But I'm only thinking of U and I,

Cutting you out my life,

Baby, that would be worse than suicide,

See, our love grows like spring flowers,

But keeps me warm like a warm summer day,

I try to play it cool,

But my stomach gets knotted up,

When you walk my way,

People can think what they want,

What you and I have,

Is only our business,

You fulfil my desires so well,

And somehow maintain my interest,

I want to honour you,

And love you,

The way that no other man can,

I want a love so dependable,

That without each other, we can't stand,

The feeling of when the bases are loaded,

And the batter is wishing for a Grand Slam,

So many distractions pop up,

But in my heart, I know us being together,

Is part of God's plan

I wish I could fly you to a private island,

Where we could have brunch and hold hands,

And I could feed you the type of cuisine,

That's only found in foreign lands

I vow to protect our love,

In a way no other can get to,

So deep in infatuation,

That I express it over instrumentals,

The truth is when our bodies touch,

It sends my central nervous system into shock,

A passion, I could never fathom,

Girl, I'm taking you with me to the top

"Because of You, Bae"

I love your sincerity,

Your smile,

Your authenticity,

Your kindness,

Your gentle spirit,

Just thinking of your cute face,

Can turn a bad day into a good one.

"No Rush"

I want to assure you that I am right by your side every step of the way, no matter what life may throw at us. I am glad we're not in a rush. I view us as a team, and I believe we bring the best out in each other. My entire goal is for you and me to share the same last name one day, and even then, I want to continue experiencing growth with you. Me without you is like sand with no beach and water, and I won't stop progressing until I become the man God destined for me to become. I appreciate your patience and loyalty more than words can express and you are the apple of my eye, Babygirl.

"I Don't Care What They Say"

I can feel their jealousy,

Their envious energy,

Mad that someone new is in my life,

Mad at the value you bring to the table and the loyalty you show me,

Yet they don't even know you, and since I've evolved, they miss the old me,

The Gerard that followed the crowd that was desperate and lonely,

I'm okay with friendships expiring especially times when they hinder your growing,

Secretly plotting, waiting for the opportune time to slander your name and sow seeds of disunity and iniquity to separate us,

Our blessing is near, and they can sense it,

It's shameful how our success makes them feel insecure to the point where I won't even mention,

Jealous of the way you make me smile,

Jealous of the way I protect and provide for you,

Somehow, they feel you being in my life means they are being replaced,

So filled with envy, its that uncomfortable yet familiar look on the face,

Humility, wisdom, and endurance,

An adequate depiction of a 'Proverbs 31' wife,

Trying to convince me the prophecy I saw was a lie,

Because they can feel our light

BENEDICTION

Benediction

When I'm with you, it's as if time stands still and nothing else matters. My mundane worries dwindle away because of the endless butterflies I feel when I'm with you. Having you in my life motivates me to change for the better, and repeatedly makes my soul smile.

Made in the USA
Columbia, SC
02 December 2024

48264011R00059